What's Your Style?

HIPSTER FASHION

KAREN LATCHANA KENNEY

Lerner Publications Company
Minneapolis

Lerner Publications Company
A division of Lerner Publishing Group, Inc.
241 First Avenue North
Minneapolis, MN 55401 U.S.A.

For reading levels and more information, look up this title at www.lernerbooks.com.

Credits: Eliza Leahy and Sara E. Hoffmann (editorial), Emily Harris (design), Giliane Mansfeldt (photos), Heidi Hogg (production).

Main body text set in Adrianna Light 12/14.
Typeface provided by Chank.

Library of Congress Cataloging-in-Publication Data

Kenney, Karen Latchana.
    Hipster fashion / by Karen Latchana Kenney ; illustrated by Ashley Newsome Kubley.
        pages   cm — (What's your style?)
    Includes index.
    ISBN 978–1–4677–1472–3 (lib. bdg. : alk. paper)
    ISBN 978–1–4677–2528–6 (eBook)
    1. Fashion. 2. Fashion design. I. Title.
TT515.K456 2014
746.9'2—dc23   2013018712

Manufactured in the United States of America
1 – PC – 12/31/13

What's Your Style?

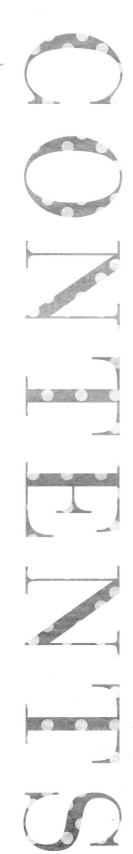

CONTENTS

Could *You*
BE A HIPSTER?

Do you have an unusual sense of style? Do quirky things appeal to you? Take this quiz to find out if hipster fashion might be your thing.

1. Your outfits are
   a. perfectly matched
   b. beachy and breezy
   c. studded, zippered, and all black
   d. a little nerdy and unexpected

2. The celeb whose style you most admire is
   a. Vanessa Hudgens
   b. Beyoncé
   c. Taylor Swift
   d. Zooey Deschanel

3. Your go-to accessory is
   a. a cozy knit cap
   b. the sickest skull ring
   c. a leather cross-body bag
   d. black-rimmed glasses

4. The perfect T-shirt is
   a. black and sparkly
   b. long and loose
   c. tie-dyed and ripped
   d. retro and ironic

5. The coolest kicks in your closet are
   a. riding boots
   b. casual sandals
   c. platform heels
   d. Converse sneakers

6. If you had to describe your personality in one word, you'd pick
   a. rocker
   b. glam
   c. earthy
   d. quirky

Did you answer mostly *d*'s? If so, you're a **hipster**! The hipster lifestyle is independent, alternative, and spunky. Hipster fashion flaunts a carefree, quirky, and ironic look.

If you didn't come up with *d*'s, hipster fashion might not be up your alley. But any fashion lover can benefit from learning about different looks. Do you want to know more about hipster style? Let's check out what makes this kitschy, cool fashion so fun to wear.

Who's Got THE LOOK?

A great way to learn about any style is to take a look at those who wear it. Lots of celebrities are into hipster fashion. From retro tees to whimsical jewelry, they've got the look mastered. And there's more than just one hipster style. These celebs experiment by mixing textures, colors, and cuts to create one-of-a-kind looks. Vintage accessories and bold colors help them fashion their own signature styles.

Who are some of the trendiest hipster stars on the scene? Let's start with . . .

EMMA WATSON

Fans know her as Hermione Granger, the nerdy, smart, and eager best friend of Harry Potter—but in real life, Emma Watson is the queen of carefree hipster style. "I have Hermione to thank, in a weird way, for my sense of style," Emma said. "Playing this role, fashion was my way of expressing myself away from that school uniform. When I got the chance to dress myself, I was so thrilled to be able to be Emma and show a different side of myself." This British actress likes to experiment by mixing textures and finding pieces of clothing with one-of-a-kind flair.

Here's how Emma makes a hipster fashion statement:

- She likes unusual details in her clothing, like asymmetrical hemlines on skirts and dresses.

- She keeps her outfits simple but spices things up with daring necklaces, bold bags, and other eye-catching accessories.

- She mixes unexpected pieces, such as a leather jacket and a floral skirt.

- She adds cute headbands and floppy hats.

Take a look at how Emma rocks her own kind of hipster-chic style.

Looking for another hipster role model? This Canadian actor is also known for his hipster fashion sense. He's got a casual, cool style that looks effortlessly put together. It's . . .

Ryan Gosling

Once a child star on the Disney Channel, Ryan Gosling has grown up to be a dreamy leading man in indie films and mainstream movies. Besides acting, he's also a director, writer, and musician.

Here's how Ryan creates his unique look:

- He's the king of V-neck cardigans—patterned, striped, or in a bold color.

- He's a fan of the plain, white tee.

- He rocks dark-rimmed glasses or stylish aviators.

- He goes for the shaggy and scruffy look, leaving his face unshaved and his hair messy.

- He sports a leather jacket to keep it cool and edgy.

See how Ryan rocks his truly unique look.

Check Out These Other Famous **Hipsters!**

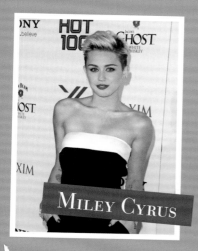

MILEY CYRUS

JOHNNY DEPP

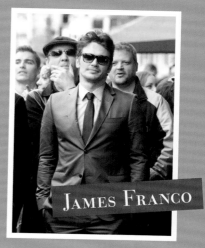

JAMES FRANCO

Styling Tip:

Make a **Hipster** Style Blog

To have your favorite hipster styles on hand, create a style blog. Look online to find hipster looks that you love. Try checking out hipster celeb photos, fashion websites, or stores that carry hipster clothing. And you can even take photos of your own hipster outfits. Pin your favorite looks to your Pinterest page. Or post your favorite looks to your Tumblr site. After a while, you'll start to see a pattern to the looks you choose. This will help you define your own hipster style. Who knows? You might even get some followers who love your hipster fashion sense!

For more inspiration, check out the super-stylish website run by fashion blogger Tavi Gevinson (right).

This next star knows how to rock hipster fashion too. She is known for her cute and unusual fashion sense with bold pops of color. Look no further than . . .

ZOOEY DESCHANEL

Popular singer and *New Girl* star Zooey Deschanel is a true retro hipster when it comes to fashion. She likes to wear vintage-inspired gems, like pretty, ruffled dresses, and pair them with cute coats or cardigans that have unique details.

How does Zooey achieve the retro vibe?

- She dons dresses with a 1950s and 1960s flair.

- She keeps her bangs long with a straight cut.

- She wears pleats and tiered ruffles.

- She adds blouses with structured Peter Pan collars.

- She adds layers of fun cardigans or brightly colored coats.

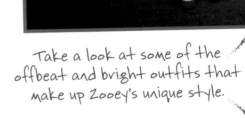

Take a look at some of the offbeat and bright outfits that make up Zooey's unique style.

Are you in search of a stylish-yet-casual hipster fashion icon? We can't forget a star who builds her look around wild prints and unexpected finds. It's Beyoncé's little sis!

SOLANGE KNOWLES

Solange's not only beautiful. She also has an awesome hipster fashion sense. How does Solange create her fashionable geek-chic ensembles?

- She wears flyaway cardigans with retro graphic patterns.

- She makes a splash in brightly patterned dresses paired with tall black boots.

- She sports short shorts and platform shoes with a 1970s vibe.

- She pulls off daring color combos like no one else we know.

What do you think of Solange's one-of-a-kind hipster vibe?

How Do I
GET THE LOOK?

Before you start pulling together carefree hipster looks, you'll need to learn a few basics. What colors are more hipster-friendly than others? What kinds of patterns and cuts should you choose? There are some simple guidelines you can follow. Take a look at these tips before you gather hipster essentials for your wardrobe.

VINTAGE CUTS

It doesn't have to *be* old. It just has to *look* old. Dresses with full skirts and small waists are great. High-waisted shorts fit this style as well. And vintage-looking patterns make for awesome outfits. Try polka dots, plaids, or florals. Don't forget T-shirts with graphics of classic rock or oldies bands, old sports teams' logos, or off-air television shows.

This quirky couple shows off vintage hipster style.

Menswear-inspired jackets bring chill yet refined structure to these hipster ensembles.

Colorful sunglasses add some fun to understated checkered tops.

BALANCE

The hipster look is all about balance. For example, to counter a feminine vintage piece, add some accessories with a masculine touch. Hats like fedoras or beanies work well. Or if your outfit is loose and flowy, add some Oxford shoes. Oxfords bring structure to any look.

Unexpected Mixes

A hipster outfit is an unexpected mix of styles. Old is mixed with new. The hipster style also blends interesting accessories, patterns, and colors. Nerdy glasses can go with a slouchy, long dress. Stripes can go with polka dots. Neon colors are welcome into a mix of earthy and neutral tones. The more unusual the outfit the better.

Unusual is the name of the game when it comes to hipster fashion.

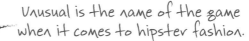

1960s

1950s

Hipster Influences

The modern hipster look pulls fashion influences from several different decades. The 1950s style inspired hipsters to don dresses with small cinched waists and feminine patterns. Fashion in the 1960s introduced the free-flowing look, simple silhouettes, and minimal accessories that many hipsters favor. The 1980s decade is to thank for the neon colors and geometric patterns commonly found in hipsters' closets. These retro influences all come together to create fantastic fashion—but hipsters add their own modern twists as well.

1980s

The sweaters worn by the cast of The Cosby Show from the 1980s fit right into the hipster's wardrobe.

Clothing

It's time to take a more in-depth look at the clothing that defines hipster style. Exactly what kinds of clothes will you need to achieve hipster coolness? These must-have pieces will become your hipster staples.

Retro Dresses

Hipster girls can look for inspiration in old television shows and movies when choosing dresses. Look especially to the 1950s and the early 1960s, when dresses were more fitted at the tops and fuller in the skirts. Try dresses with a sweetheart neckline or a pretty collar at the top. Look for unusual patterns or fabrics, like florals, lace, or even wild leopard. If it catches your eye off the rack with a pop of color or a surprising pattern, it is sure to do the trick!

SKINNY JEANS

Both guys and girls can get plenty of wear out of a good pair of skinny jeans. You can go for a dark tone or try a bright color instead. Skinny jeans come in every color, so you have a lot of options! Try bright purple or red for a spunky look. Patterned jeans are eye-catching too. Try vintage-looking florals (think Grandma's tablecloth!), colorful designs, splattered paint, or acid-wash. Roll the bottoms of the pant legs up for a cuffed, on-the-go look.

Mary J. Blige (above) and actor Freida Pinto (left) know how to rock skinny jeans.

UNIQUE TEES

Make a statement with your tee! Say something ironic or funny. Pick one with a silly image, like a unicorn galloping over a rainbow. Or try one with a sassy saying, like "The bands I listen to don't even have band names yet." Old band tour shirts or television show graphics (think *The Smurfs* or *The Simpsons*) work well too. If it's funny, strange, and a little outdated, it'll be great!

Bring on the Layers

Layering is part of hipster style as well. Blazers give a more structured look to a flowy dress or top. They also add some polish to a faded tee. Cardigans are in the closet of almost every hipster. Oversized V-necks with buttons fit nicely over skinny jeans. You'll want to grab some patterned sweaters too. Try ones with zigzags, geometric shapes, or something unexpected like teddy bears in the design. And if you want to wear your cutoffs in the fall, girls can just throw some patterned tights on underneath.

MIX & MATCH

You've got the hipster musts. You just need to figure out how to mix and match those pieces. You know you can pair fitted layers with oversized items to bring a little structure to your outfit. Here are a few more tips for getting a great hipster mix:

- Pair dresses with sneakers. Wear suspenders with casual skinny jeans. You need a good balance of traditional and quirky for that unexpected-looking outfit.

- Mix patterns with solids or contrasting patterns. Put stripes with plaids or florals with polka dots. Experiment to see what looks unique. Maybe you have a moss-green cardigan that will go well with a polka-dotted white and blue tank. Look in your closet for pieces you've never thought to combine before!

- Add pops of bright color. Use colors in unexpected ways, like in tights, shoes, or sunglasses.

- Scour thrift stores for truly one-of-a-kind finds. A vintage cardigan becomes super hip when paired with orange jeans and a fedora hat.

Now that you've got some quirky clothes, you need the perfect shoes. The right kicks are key to mastering hipster fashion. Check out some must-have choices in the next chapter to add to your hipster vibe.

Cute Cutoffs

Cutoff jean shorts make a great hipster look for summertime! You don't need to buy them at a store. Make your own with a pair of old jeans instead.

What you need:

- an old pair of high-waisted jeans

- a black marker

- a measuring tape or a ruler (optional)

- scissors

- tweezers

What you do:

1. Get a parent's permission to use the old pair of high-waisted jeans that you found. Make sure the parent knows that you'll be cutting the jeans!

2. Grab the marker and put on the jeans. Stand in front of a mirror. Use the marker to mark where you want to cut off your pants. You might want to use a measuring tape or a ruler to help you draw a straight line.

3. Take off the jeans, and cut them with the scissors. Be sure to follow the marker lines!

4. Fold the jean shorts in half so that the leg openings are touching. Make sure the legs are evenly cut. If one side is too long, trim it to match the other side.

5. Fray the ends by pulling on the white threads with the tweezers.

6. Trim the frayed ends with your scissors. You will probably have to trim the ends again after you wash and dry your cutoffs.

7. Throw on a flannel shirt or a fun tank top, and show off your new cutoffs!

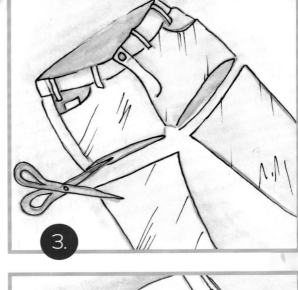

3.

EVEN UP the LENGTH...

4.

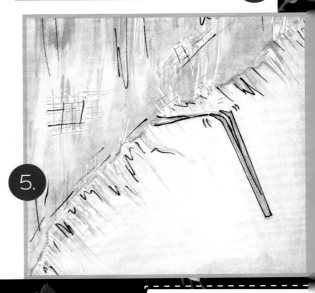

5.

SHOES

When it comes to hipster style, stilettos don't really fit in. Hipsters like to walk or ride bikes to get around, so comfortable shoes are important. Many hipster shoes have a very masculine touch—even girls' shoes. Some have a vintage feel. Let's check out the different types of shoes that define hipster fashion.

Psy looks stylish in his oxfords!

OXFORDS

These laced leather shoes look like they should go with a three-pieced suit. Feminine versions of Oxfords may add a bit of a heel. They can also have simple designs punched into the leather, or they can look supermodern with bold, bright colors.

TV personality and fashion designer whitney Port rocks some stylish sneaks in this photo op.

Sneakers

Casual sneakers are hipster essentials. They look great with skinny jeans and dresses too. Converse low- or high-tops are a common choice, but any simple sneaker will do. Go for white, neon, or a funky color combo. A galaxy pattern, leopard print, or kitschy-looking design like an old cartoon can also be fun with this look.

FLATS

Flats are an excellent option for hipster girls. Cool colors are what make flats fit hipster fashion. Neon yellow and bright turquoise are great choices. A little bling is fun too. Look for sequins or sparkles. Canvas flats are another hipster staple.

LEATHER BOOTS

Leather boots add some tough-looking style to a hipster outfit. Think Dr. Martens, motorcycle boots, or combat boots. Girls can pair boots with tights and socks to go with flowy dresses. Leather boots can even be worn with shorts in warm weather. In cooler weather, boots go great with oversized wool socks that can be seen above the tops of boots.

Galaxy Shoes

Turn black canvas into a swirling, cosmic galaxy for the coolest-looking shoes.

What you need:

- black canvas shoes

- duct tape

- acrylic paint in galaxy-like colors (purple, blue, pink, white, and yellow are some must-haves)

- a piece of cardboard

- newspaper

- a sponge

- a small paintbrush

What you do:

1. If your shoes have laces, remove them. Put the duct tape on the soles of the shoes. This stops paint from getting on the shoe bottoms.

2. Make a pallet of colors on the cardboard. These will be the colors of your galaxy.

3. Lay the newspaper on your workspace to keep splatters to a minimum.

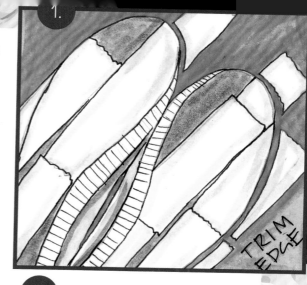

4. Get one color on the sponge. You can make random splotches or loose shapes—like swirls—if you prefer. The shoe is your personal canvas, so feel free to have fun!

5. Start adding more splotches or shapes in different colors. Check out some space photos if you want to see how galaxies look so you can try to give your shoe a similar appearance. But just remember that it's better if it's imperfect.

6. Repeat with the other shoe, and then let the shoes dry for around 30 minutes.

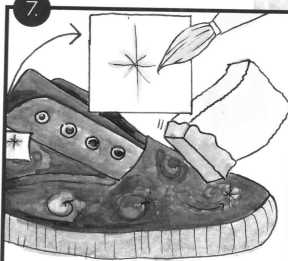

7. Use the small paintbrush and yellow or white paint. Add tiny stars to your galaxies. Keep them simple, with just lines that cross at a center point.

8. Wait for your shoes to completely dry. Lace them up if you like, and pair them with some skinny jeans or a flowy skirt with a belt for a far-out look.

Styling Tip:

What if painting's not your thing? Then head outside with your pallet, and try just splattering some paint onto your shoes. Use different colors and fling the paint. It might be a little messy, but it has a great result!

ACCESSORIES

Want to quickly change up an outfit and get a whole new look? Just switch your accessories. Be playful and bold—with hipster accessories you can have a lot of fun. Quirky jewelry, glasses, scarves, hats, and bags all create different hipster vibes. Take a look at the many ways accessories can truly jazz up your outfits and show your unique hipster style.

NECKLACES, RINGS, AND EARRINGS

Owls, hearts, horses, and kitschy designs show up on hipster necklaces, rings, and earrings—especially those designed for hipster girls. Wear long pendants with charms. Birds, bikes, and clocks make cool pendants. A simple geometric shape can be a funky addition. Spice things up with spiky bracelets and rings in bright colors.

As for earrings, little studs are great. Look for ones with a unique shape. Try hearts, cameras, bows, or even mustaches. If it's unusual and unexpected, that makes it even better.

Socks

Wear socks, even when it might seem strange. Wear them under sandals for a nerd-chic look. Wearing socks with ankle boots communicates a carefree vibe. Layer them and make them slouchy or pull them all the way up to your knees. Knee-highs look great with a pair of cutoff shorts.

NERDY GLASSES

Think of the classic nerd glasses. Thick and chunky frames with black rims are perfect for the hipster look, and some bold color works too. Some daring hipsters go for the Harry Potter-style circular glasses. And you don't need a prescription to get them. You can find fake glasses just about anywhere.

SCARVES, SCARVES, SCARVES!

Want some instant hipster cred? Wrap a fringed scarf around your neck. Just make sure the pointed ends are in the front. But other scarves work well too. They can be long and thin, have multiple strands, or be thick and chunky. Pair them with T-shirts for a fun, relaxed look.

MENSWEAR HATS

These hats work well for both guys and girls. Think retro fedoras and slouchy beanies. Wide-brimmed Panama hats add a fun touch as well. For the ladies, a good menswear-inspired hat balances a girly-hipster outfit and jewelry.

HIPSTER BAGS

A messenger bag or an oversized, slouchy bag completes your outfit. These bags are big enough to hold your hipster essentials, and they work well when biking or walking. For a really retro look, wear a fanny pack. Fanny packs are small pouches with zippers that are usually strapped around the waist. Sporting one of these will take you straight back to the late 1980s.

Check out this model's fanny pack.

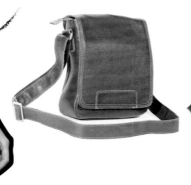

Hipster Scarf

Old T-shirts make the coolest scarves. These scarves are easy to pull off too. Check out how to do it!

What you need:

- a few cotton T-shirts in different colors (find ones without side seams or ribs if you can)

- scissors

What you do:

1. Lay a T-shirt out on a table. Make sure it is flat.

2. Cut the hem off and throw it away. (The hem is the stitching that goes around the bottom of the shirt.)

3. Starting at the bottom of the T-shirt, cut 1-inch (2.5-centimeter) strips across from one side to the other until you reach the armholes.

3.

STOP HERE

4. Grab a bunch of strips. Pull gently on the ends of the strips to stretch them out. Once they are stretched out, grab another bunch of strips and do the same thing until all the strips are stretched out.

5. Complete steps 1 to 4 again with another T-shirt in a different color. Repeat with each of your Ts.

6. Now it's time to start getting really creative. If you want a multicolored scarf, grab some different colored strips and try putting them around your neck at once. If you want single-colored scarves, put strips of just one color around your neck and save the others for another time. If you want a scarf with a little bling, try pairing the strips with pretty beaded or jeweled necklaces. The possibilities are endless!

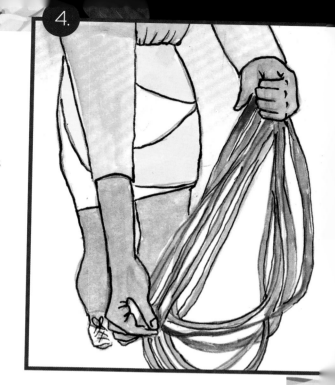

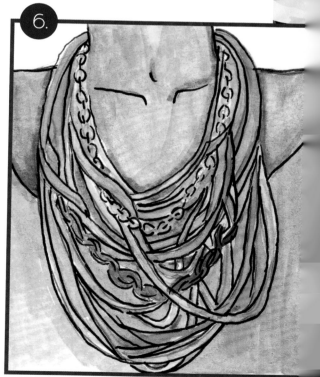

HAIR AND MAKEUP

Once your clothes, shoes, and accessories are set to go, it's time to turn to hair and—for those who are into it—makeup. Hipsters have a mostly natural look with some bold pops of color. Different hairstyles are fun ways to experiment. Check out these hair and makeup ideas to complete your hipster look.

UNUSUAL NAILS

This one applies more to girls than to guys—and many hipster girls might want to leave their nails au naturel. Remember: a hipster's look is never overdone. But if you're up for a mani, there are lots of ways to do your nails that speak to hipster style. As you might have guessed, you won't find pretty pastels or soft reds on a hipster girl's hands. Think neon green and backward French tips instead. Grays, blues, and muted neutrals are popular hipster polish choices. Funky designs are in too. Try chevrons, stripes, or polka dots. You can even get a galaxy design on your nails!

Natural Face and Bright Lips

Think minimal when it comes to face and eye makeup. No makeup at all is great. Or just use mineral foundation on your face and a little earth-toned eyeliner to define your eyes. Browns or other neutral colors work best. You can add a pretty natural lip gloss or—if you're feeling bold—add a simple pop of color with bright red lipstick.

Cassie sports the shaved look.

HIPSTER HAIRCUTS

Short, cropped haircuts are popular with hipster girls. Such cuts can be worn swept to the side. Or you can spike them up. This kind of cut looks especially cute with a super-girly dress.

Another look for girls is to go boyish on one side and all-girl on the other. For this look, one side of the head is cut very short, almost shaved. The rest of the hair is longer and carefree. Check out Rihanna and singer/model Cassie, who've both had the half-shaved hairstyle.

For guys, the latest hipster hair is an undercut. This hairstyle is very short or shaved on the sides but is kept longer on top. The long hair on top can be slicked back or neatly combed to the side.

LONG AND CAREFREE

Both girls and guys can pull off the free and easy look defined by long, unruly locks. Just let your hair grow, and keep it messy. It's as simple as that! Use your fingers or a wide-tooth comb to untangle any snarls, though.

Celebs China Anne McClain (left) and Rachel McAdams (below, left) have both sported dip-dyed hair.

Dip-Dyed and Funky Colors

Another surprising look is dip-dyed, or ombre, hair. This one's more common for girls, but daring guys can try it out as well. (Both guys and girls should check with a parent before breaking out the dye!) Dip-dyed hair is a look where the ends of the hair gradually go from one color to another. The colors might be browns and blonds that get darker or lighter from the roots to the tips of your hair. Unusual colors are popular too. Some people try blues and purples. Others even add streaks of gray!

If dip-dyed hair isn't your thing, you might try a fun all-over color instead. Blues, pinks, reds, and purples make a super-fun hipster look.

Top Knots

A simple and stylish hairdo for hipster girls is the top knot, or high bun. It's kind of nerdy but classic as well. Simply pull your hair to the top of your head. Fold one end over so there's a knob of hair sticking up. Put a ponytail holder around the knob. Then twist the long loose end around the knob to make a bun. Tuck the tip of the loose end into your bun and you're done!

Super-Easy (and Temporary!) Dip Dye

Don't want to dye your hair permanently? Try hair chalking instead. It gives you a temporary dip dye, and it's pretty simple to do. (As with any drastic hair change, though, make sure to check with a parent before you give this a try.) The color will wash out after two to three shampoos.

What you need:

- latex gloves

- old towels

- a spray bottle filled with water

- soft pastels (these can be found in art supply stores)

- a curling iron set on low heat

What you do:

1. Put on your latex gloves, and drape one of the old towels around your neck. You may want to set a towel down under the pastels too.

2. Pull out a small section of hair. Spray it with water so that it is damp.

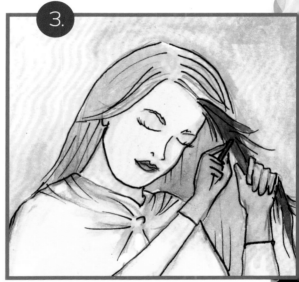

3. Pick a pastel and hold the hair section tight. Rub the pastel toward the ends of your hair. Do this a few times until you see the color catch on your hair.

4. Curl the hair section with a curling iron to set the color. If some color gets on the curling iron, wipe it off.

5. Make as many color sections as you like. Just repeat steps 1 to 4. Then enjoy your colorful locks!

Your HIPSTER Look

Hipster fashion is all about showing your quirky and surprising style—from your purple ombre hair to your nerdy glasses. You've learned about the basic elements of the look. But how will *you* use those elements? There are no definite rules. It is completely up to you!

So what kind of hipster look will you go for? Will you be retro cool like Zooey Deschanel or geek chic like Solange Knowles? Maybe you'll channel Ryan Gosling and go with a cool and casual look. Just remember, make it eclectic. Play around with your clothes. And don't think too hard about it. Fashion is all about having fun with how you look and what you wear. What style will you rock today? Just check out your closet, look in the mirror, and find out!

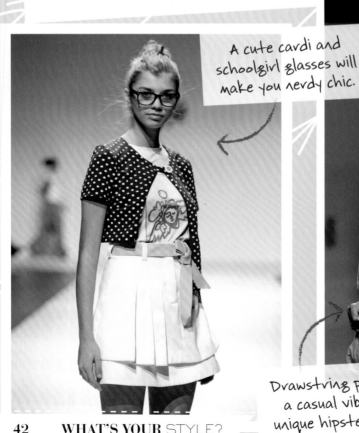

A cute cardi and schoolgirl glasses will make you nerdy chic.

Drawstring pants bring a casual vibe to this unique hipster ensemble.

Casual hipsters strut their stuff.

Dressier hipsters look set for a night on the town.

HIPSTER RESOURCES

Do you want to learn more about being a hipster? Check out these ideas:

Where to Find Hipster Stuff

- Look in vintage and thrift stores for rocker tees, 1950s and 1960s dresses and skirts, and dark- or thick-rimmed glasses. Just bring your vintage glasses with you next time you get your vision checked and have the doctor put in the kind of lenses you need.

- Check out a record store for some newer band tees. Buy a few records while you're there too. Good music on old-fashioned vinyl is another hipster essential.

- Go to estate and garage sales and antique stores for interesting jewelry.

Where to Find Hipster Fashion Inspiration and Tutorials

- Look for hair, makeup, and clothing tutorials on YouTube.

- Find fashion inspiration on Tumblr or Pinterest sites.

- Read crafting blogs to find ways to make hipster scarves and cutoffs.

- Page through some music magazines like *Rolling Stone* or *Clash* to learn about hipster music, culture, and lifestyle.

Hipster Songs to Check Out

- "Graceless" by the National
- "Little Numbers" by Boy
- "Ho Hey" by the Lumineers
- "Never Wanted Your Love" by She & Him

What to Watch to Get in the Hipster Spirit

- Indie films like *Moonrise Kingdom* or *The Perks of Being a Wallflower*
- Oldie but goodie TV shows like *The Fresh Prince of Bel-Air* or *Saved by the Bell*

GLOSSARY

asymmetrical: having parts that are not equal, such as the hem of a skirt that is longer on one side

chevron: a line or a stripe in the shape of a V or an upside-down V

eclectic: a word to describe a person or a thing that draws from many different sources. For example, a person with an eclectic fashion sense might draw his or her sense of style from several different time periods or cultures.

fedora: a low soft felt hat with the crown creased lengthwise

ironic: a word to describe something—such as a fashion or a saying—that is strange or funny because it's unexpected. For example, a teenager who no longer watches cartoons might wear a cartoon-themed shirt to be ironic.

kitschy: a word to describe art, design, or fashion that is generally thought to be ugly or too cutesy but is appreciated in an ironic way

ombre: a gradual color change in fabric or hair, where one end is much darker than the other

Panama hat: a wide-brimmed hat, typically woven from straw

pendant: a hanging ornament, such as on a necklace

Peter Pan collar: a collar on a shirt or dress that lays flat against the torso and has rounded edges

quirky: to have strange or unusual traits

silhouette: the shape of something, such as a dress

vintage: from the past

SOURCE NOTE

7. Vanessa Lawrence, "Emma Watson Set Free," *Women's Wear Daily,* November 19, 2010, http://www.wwd.com/eye/people/emma-watson-set-free-3385628.

Further Information

Higgins, Nadia. *Emma Watson: From Wizards to Wallflowers.* **Minneapolis: Lerner Publications, 2014.**
Learn more about Emma Watson in this fun bio documenting her rise to fame.

Shoket, Ann. *Seventeen Ultimate Guide to Style: How to Find Your Perfect Look.* **Philadelphia: Running Press, 2011.**
Not sure if hipster or another style is best for you? Then look to this helpful book to guide you!

Teen Vogue
http://www.teenvogue.com
Check out this site for the latest in hipster and other fashion styles.

Thomas, Isabel. *Being a Fashion Stylist.* **Minneapolis: Lerner Publications, 2013.**
Ever wondered what it's like to work as a fashion stylist? This book is the perfect find for aspiring fashionistas!

Walker, Jackie. *Expressionista: How to Express your True Self through (and Despite) Fashion.* **New York: Aladdin, 2013.**
This title will help you discover your fashion persona and set up a closet to reflect your sense of style.

Waxman, Laura Hamilton. *Fabulous Fashion Inventions.* **Minneapolis: Lerner Publications, 2014.**
Read about the strange, interesting, and amazing inventions that have changed the fashion world throughout the years.

Index

PHOTO ACKNOWLEGMENTS

The images in this book are used with the permission of: © Yusuf Doganay/Shutterstock, p. 3; © Ericlefrancais/Bigstock, p. 4; © Zlatko Kostic/Vetta/Getty Images, p. 5 (top); © Masson/Shutterstock, pp. 5 (bottom), 13 (middle right); © Marc Piasecki/WireImage/Getty Images, p. 6; © Donato Sardella/WireImage/Getty Images, pp. 7 (left), 43 (top left); DVS iPhoto Inc./Newscom, p. 7 (middle); © Andy Kropa/Getty Images, p. 7 (right); © Tony Barson Archive/WireImage/Getty Images, p. 8 (top); © John Sciulli/WireImage/Getty Images, p. 8 (bottom left); © J. Vespa/WireImage/Getty Images, p. 8 (bottom right); © S_bukley/Shutterstock, p. 9 (top); © Phil Stafford/Shutterstock, p. 9 (right middle); © Helga Esteb/Shutterstock, p. 9 (left middle); © Rabbani and Solimene Photography/Getty Images, p. 9 (bottom); © Fox/Getty Images, p. 10 (top); © Jeffrey Mayer/WireImage/Getty Images, p. 10 (bottom left); © Jason LaVeris/FilmMagic/Getty Images, pp. 10 (bottom middle), 38 (top left); © Alberto E. Rodriguez/Getty Images, p. 10 (bottom right); © FilmMagic/Getty Images, p. 11 (top); © Mike Lawrie/Getty Images, p. 11 (bottom left); © Jacopo Raule/WireImage/Getty Images, p. 11 (bottom right); © A J Cotton/Dreamstime, p. 12 (bottom left); © Verity Jane Smith/Botanica/Getty Images, p. 12 (bottom right); © iStockphoto/timnewman, p. 13 (top left); © Willee Cole/Bigstock, p. 13 (top right); © Comstock Images/Getty Images, p. 13 (bottom left); © Nito/Bigstock, p. 14 (top left); © iStockphoto/Kurt Paris, p. 14 (top right); © WIN-Initiative/Getty Images, p. 14 (bottom left); © iStockphoto/Goldmund Lukic, p. 14 (bottom right); © iofoto/Bigstock, p. 15 (background); © Christopher Ames/E+/Getty Images, p. 15 (top left); © Iofoto/Dreamstime, p. 15 (top right); © Alan Singer/NBC/NBCU Photo Bank/Getty Images, p. 15 (bottom); © Sadie Roberts/Workbook Stock/Getty Images, p. 16 (left); © Kedrov/Shutterstock, p. 16 (middle); © Karkas/Shutterstock, pp. 16 (right), 19 (middle), 19 (bottom middle), 23 (bottom middle); © FeatureFlash/Shutterstock, pp. 17 (top left), 36 (top); © Ben Pruchnie/FilmMagic/Getty Images, p. 17 (top right); © Alexander Image/Shutterstock, p. 17 (middle); © Gareth Cattermole/Getty Images, p. 17 (bottom middle); © Todd Strand/Independent Picture Service, pp. 17 (top middle), 17 (bottom left), 17 (bottom right), 28 (bottom left), 28 (bottom middle), 28 (bottom right); © iStockphoto/chrisgramly, p. 18 (top left); © ImageSource/Getty Images, p. 18 (top right); © Jupiterimages/Workbook Stock/Getty Images, p. 18 (bottom left); © Shelby Jean Gates/Workbook Stock/Getty Images, p. 18 (bottom right); © Evikka/Shutterstock, p. 19 (top right); © Buturlimov Paul/Shutterstock, p. 19 (bottom right); © Lucy Liu/Shutterstock, p. 19 (bottom left); © Gilbert Carrasquillo/FilmMagic/Getty Images, p. 22 (top); © Balefire/Shutterstock, p. 22 (middle left); © Ablestock/Thinkstock, p. 22 (bottom left); Tom Wallace/Minneapolis Star Tribune/Newscom, p. 22 (bottom right); © BCFC/Bigstock, p. 23 (top left); © Buffy1982/Dreamstime, p. 23 (top right); © Charley Gallay/WireImage/Getty Images, p. 23 (middle left); © Jocic/Bigstock, p. 23 (middle right); © iStockphoto/Pearleye, p. 23 (bottom left); © Capa34/Bigstock, p. 24 (top left); © Photobac/Shutterstock, p. 24 (top right); © iStockphoto/Thinkstock, p. 24 (bottom left), 13 (bottom right); © Elnur/Bigstock, p. 25 (top right), 34 (middle); © Kletr/Shutterstock, p. 25 (top); © Irina1977/Shutterstock, p. 25 (bottom left); © Squirrelli/Dreamstime, p. 28 (top); © RuslanOmega/Bigstock, p. 29 (top); © Nata Sha/Shutterstock, p. 29 (bottom left); © JupiterImages/Brand X Pictures/Thinkstock, p. 29 (middle right); © Jayme Thorton/Stone/Getty Images, p. 29 (bottom right); © Catwalker/Shutterstock, pp. 29 (middle left), 31 (bottom left), 42 (right), 43 (top right), 43 (bottom left); © iStockphoto/Stolenpencil, p. 30 (background); © Alys Tomlinson/Taxi/Getty Images, p. 30 (top left); © Brook Pifer/Taxi/Getty Images, p. 30 (top right); © Luba V Nel/Shutterstock, p. 30 (bottom left); © Wavebreakmedia/Shutterstock, p. 30 (bottom right); © Blueskies9/Bigstock, p. 31 (top); © Andrej Godjevac/E+/Getty Images, p. 31 (middle center), 39 (bottom right); © Bevan Goldswain/Dreamstime, p. 31 (middle right); © Neddog/Dreamstime, p. 31 (bottom center); © Nito/Shutterstock, p. 31 (bottom right); © Foonia/Shutterstock, p. 34 (top); © FrameAngel/Shutterstock, p. 34 (bottom); © Voronin76/Shutterstock, p. 35 (top); © Dzina Belskaya/Shutterstock, p. 35 (middle left); © Mirela Bk/Shutterstock, p. 35 (middle right); © iStockphoto/iconogenic, p. 35 (bottom right); © Kubais/Shutterstock, p. 35 (bottom left); © Lunamarina/Dreamstime, p. 36 (middle); © Rido/Shutterstock, p. 36 (bottom left); © Nick David/Taxi/Getty Images, p. 36 (bottom right); © Aleshyn_Andrei/Shutterstock, p. 37; © Augustino/Shutterstock, p. 37 (inset left); © Rgbspace/Dreamstime, p. 37 (inset right); © Paul A. Herbet/Getty Images, p. 38 (top right); © Dimitrios Kambouris/Getty Images, p. 38 (bottom left); © Paul Smith/FeatureFlash/Shutterstock, p. 38 (bottom middle); © iStockphoto/Aleksandar Nakic, p. 38 (bottom right); © Alejandro Rivera/E+/Getty Images, p. 39 (top left); © MASH/Photodisc/Thinkstock, p. 39 (top right); © Paul Matthew Photography/Shutterstock, p. 39 (bottom left); © Gordana Sermek/Shutterstock, p. 42 (left); © Kristin Sinclair/FilmMagic/Getty Images, pp. 43 (middle), 43 (bottom right).

Backgrounds: © Tukkki/Dreamstime, p. 1; © Nataliia Kucherenko/Shutterstock, p. 2; © Gudinny/Shutterstock, pp. 4–5; © Ashley Mcginty/Shutterstock, pp. 6–7; © Cherry Blossom Girl/Bigstock, p. 8; © Olga Korneeva/Shutterstock pp. 10–11; Kenee/Shutterstock, p. 12; © Sniegirova Mariia/Shutterstock, p. 14; © iofoto/Bigstock, p. 15; © Radiocat/Shutterstock, p. 16; © Aleksey Vl B/Shutterstock, pp. 20–21, 26–27, 32–33, 40–41; © Vector Ninja/Shutterstock, p. 25; © iStockphoto/Stolenpencil, p. 30; © Alisa Foytik/Bigstock, pp. 42–43; © Sniegirova Mariia/Shutterstock, pp. 44–45, 46–47, 48.

Front Cover: © Sniegirova Mariia/Shutterstock (polka dots); © Ashley Mcginty/Shutterstock (floral background); © Willee Cole/Bigstock (fedora hat); © Lucy Liu/Shutterstock (sailor shirt); © Nito/Bigstock (glasses); © Kedrov/Shutterstock (vintage summer dress); © iStockphoto/Thinkstock (sneakers); © Karkas/Shutterstock (gray skirt); © Comstock Images/Getty Images (saddle shoes) © Todd Strand/Independent Picture Service (owl pendant).

Back Cover: © Olga Korneeva/Shutterstock (rose background); © Ablestock/Thinkstock (wingtip shoes); © Karkas/Shutterstock (fashion dress).

2008
Merry Christmas,
Kirsten!

Love,
Santa.

Where the Whales Sing

Victor Kelleher

Illustrations by Vivienne Goodman

Stoddart

First published in Canada in 1994 by
Stoddart Publishing Co. Limited
34 Lesmill Road, Toronto, Canada, M3B 2T6

First published by Penguin Books Australia, 1994
1 3 5 7 9 10 8 6 4 2

Typeset in 14 pt Perpetua by Midland Typesetters, Maryborough, Victoria
Made and printed in Australia by Australian Print Group, Maryborough, Victoria

Canadian Cataloguing in Publication Data

Kelleher, Victor, 1939–
Where the whales sing

ISBN 0-7737-2804-X

1. Humpback whale – Juvenile fiction. I. Title.

PZ10.3.K45Wh 1994 182.3 C94-930 464-6

Where the Whales Sing

Also by Victor Kelleher

Forbidden Paths of Thual
The Hunting of Shadroth
Master of the Grove
Papio
Taronga
The Green Piper
The Makers
Baily's Bones
The Red King
Brother Night
Del-Del
To the Dark Tower
Voices from the River
The Traveller
The Beast of Heaven
Em's Story
Wintering
Micky Darlin'

I shall sleep, and move with the moving ships,
    Change as the winds change, veer in the tide.

A. C. SWINBURNE,
The Triumph of Time

For Leila

V.K.

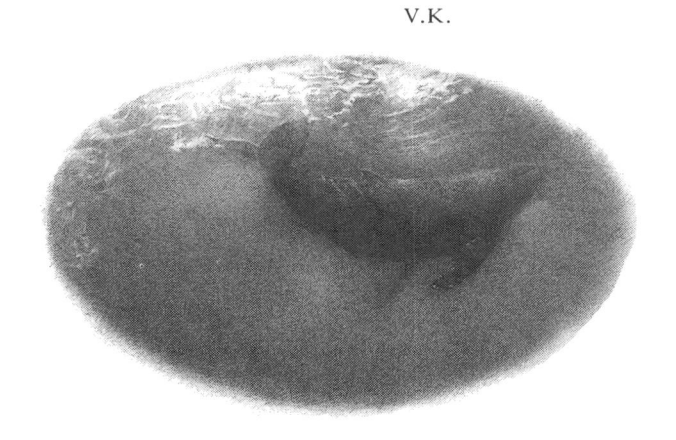

For my father

V.G.

CHAPTER ONE

Adrift

◈

CLAIRE PEERED THROUGH the wind and rain, hoping for a better view. The boat, pitching and swaying beneath her, had ploughed down into a foam-streaked trough, so she had to bide her time. But as it rode up the next wave, the sail straining above her head, she saw it again: a jet-like spout of vapour shooting skywards; exactly the kind of spout made by the great humpback whales when they surfaced.

'There!' she cried, turning to her father who was standing in the cockpit beside her, both hands clenched about the wheel.

He brought his mouth close to her ear. 'Probably just spray,' he shouted. 'No good now anyway. Too rough.'

He was already turning the wheel, the sails rattling as the boat swung around and settled to a new course that would take them back to Sydney.

1

'But I saw it!' she insisted, shouting through the noise of the rising gale.

He shook his head, raindrops cascading from his chin and nose. 'Can't see anything in this,' he roared. 'Have to try again next year.'

Next year! The disappointment of it struck her more harshly than the wind. For weeks she had prepared for this trip; read everything she could about humpback whales; persuaded her father to give up a precious weekend's yacht-racing to bring her out here – all in the hope of sighting one of the migratory pods heading south for the summer. And here they were, beaten by the weather. With the dismal prospect of a whole year's waiting before they could try again.

'Please, Dad,' she began, 'can't we just look for a bit . . . ?'

She broke off as the boat suddenly bucked like a live animal. The violence of the movement hurled her from the cockpit and half-over the side. As she dangled there, held only by her safety harness, she spied a mountainous black shape curving past below. Then the boat was struck again, so hard that with a lurching roll it turned right over.

She realised what had happened even as she was dragged down. One of the whales she had glimpsed earlier had surfaced directly beneath them. She thought desperately: I'm going to drown! For black water was streaming past her face; more of it filling her mouth and nose, threatening to suffocate her. Struggling made no difference. The noise and the rush of water went on just the same. All she could do was hold on to the breath that was trying to burst out of her; keep her teeth clenched shut until, with another lurching tug, she was hauled up into the murky light and wind.

She found she was back in the cockpit again, standing knee-deep in water. The rest of the boat was in a state of ruin: the mast down; the mainsail, like the twisted, broken wing of a giant bird, floating alongside; the narrow decks running with water and half-buried under a tangle of wires and ropes.

'Dad!' she wailed.

And saw him immediately – his head and shoulders bobbing on a nearby swell of wave. He was struggling to reach the sail, but every stroke he took only seemed to draw him further away.

She tore the lifebelt from the side of the cockpit and threw it towards him, the way she had been taught. It would have been a good throw if it had not been for the wind, which lifted it and sent it careering off in the wrong direction.

The boat rolled sluggishly, as though about to turn over once again; and while she still had the chance she unclipped her harness, pulled open the hatch, and slid down into the cabin. There was water down there too, ankle-deep and cluttered with pots and pans that slopped noisily from side to side. Working hurriedly, and mainly by feel, she located the inflatable life-raft, stowed beneath one of the bunks, and heaved it up the ladder.

Her father was further away from the boat now, and downwind. He waved to her as she reappeared and shouted words she could not make out.

'It's all right, I'm coming!' she called back, and jerked the cord on the life-raft.

It inflated with unexpected speed. There was a sharp hiss of gas, and it squirmed like a living creature beneath her hands, growing magically into a canopied raft that was too large for the cockpit. She tried to steady it as it snapped out to its full extent, but the wind gusted strongly, spilling it over the side and tearing it from her grasp.

She seriously considered following it. Crouched at the stern, she readied herself to jump, hesitated, and finally held back – because the wind was spinning the raft away far more quickly than she could swim. Sitting high on the swells, it drifted straight towards her father. Thankfully, she saw him catch at its trailing rope and curl one arm over its inflated side; but before he could haul himself in under the canopy, a squall of rain swept down and he disappeared from view.

She could not believe at first what had happened to her. She, completely alone on a damaged boat in the middle of a storm! It was the kind of thing she had never even dreamed of; and for a while she stood there helpless, staring miserably through the billowing curtains of rain.

She was forced into action by the stinging impact of a wave breaking over her. Fully alert, she looked about her, assessing the situation.

Despite the water in the cabin, the boat itself was still riding well. What was hampering it, making it wallow dangerously in the troughs, was the shattered mast and rigging hanging over one side. If the boat were to survive, they had to be cut away; and with that in mind, she reached under the cockpit seat and detached the axe that was clipped there.

Closing the hatch, to keep out any more water, she crawled forward across the cabin roof. The wooden mast, she now saw, had snapped off fairly cleanly. Only some splinters of wood still attached it to its base, and these she chopped through with a few blows of the axe. Next, she set about disconnecting the thin steel cables that had held it in position. She was clinging to the rail when she undid the last of them, expecting the mast to slip easily over the side and float away. Instead, it swung towards

5

her, knocking her down and crushing her leg hard against the rail post.

There was a tearing pain in her knee, so intense that for a few seconds she blacked out. When she came to, the mast was gone and another squall of rain was beating into her face. Grasping the heaving rail, she hauled herself up; but the slightest weight on her wounded leg made her feel sick and dizzy. Even the action of crawling back along the deck sent jabs of pain shooting up her thigh.

Huddled in the cockpit, shivering as much from shock and pain as from fear, she gazed forlornly out over the wind-tossed water, hoping for a glimpse of the life-raft. But all she saw through the drift of rain was a shiny black mound that might have been a whale, and might as easily have been a wave.

Dejected, fighting back tears, she re-opened the hatch. With the sail gone, there was no point in trying to steer. From now on the boat would follow its own course, regardless of anything she might do. Her only choice was to trust herself to the sea.

It was that thought which drove her below, as far as she could get from the black hillocks of water that loomed over the stern, as though about to topple down and crush her. Groaning because of the pain in her leg, she lowered herself into the cabin and closed the hatch behind her. In the darkness, water and unseen objects slopped around her feet. The wooden planking of the hull creaked and groaned. But loudest of all was the wind: like a lone wolf of the sea, it howled at the oncoming night.

In a feeble attempt to escape from it, she clambered onto one of the bunks and pulled a damp sleeping-bag over her head. It merely muffled the sound, reducing it to the voice of her own terror. She matched it with her sobbing cries; a faint whimpering that grew gradually softer and eventually stopped.

Oddly, for the boat continued to toss wildly to and fro, her sleep was deep and restful. Only once in the course of the night did she almost wake. For a minute or two the howling of the wind broke through the silence and entered her dream. Yet it failed to alarm her. In the dream, strangely, it mingled with the singing of whales: a low murmurous song that rose from the mysterious depths and whispered wordlessly to her of companionship and comfort.

CHAPTER TWO

Up from the Deep

◈

CHINKS OF SUNLIGHT showed at the edges of the hatch; and the only sounds were the creaking of the boat and the slosh of water across the floor. Foolishly, she swung herself straight out of the bunk, causing the pain in her knee and thigh to return with a rush. Again she almost blacked out and had to cling onto the bunk to prevent herself from falling.

When her vision and her breathing steadied, she groped her way to the ladder, opened the hatch, and dragged herself up into the sunlight. Although the sea was still running high, the wind had dropped and the sky was a clear, uniform blue. As the boat drifted up onto one of the crests, she swept her eyes around the horizon, hoping for a sight of land or a glimpse of some passing vessel. But the white-capped sea was empty; and over to the west there was not even a smudge of grey to mark the Australian coastline.

She nearly started to cry again then and had to press her hands to her eyes to stop any tears escaping. They'll be looking for me by now, she told herself silently. In planes and boats and everything. They'll be sure to find me by nightfall.

She went on repeating that message to herself throughout the day. Sometimes she muttered the words aloud, to ward off loneliness and to keep her mind off the dull pain in her leg. For a while she believed so completely in what she was saying that she did not budge from the cockpit in case she missed some passing boat or plane. By mid afternoon, however, she was less sure; and she took time off to go below for a drink and to collect a tin of food from the emergency supplies.

The sea, meanwhile, had grown calmer, and for that reason much emptier. Back in the cockpit, eating beans from the tin, she was less eager to scan the horizon. There seemed little point. Also, she felt too hot to go on searching – far hotter than the spring sunshine warranted.

I must be sickening for something, she thought vaguely, and she peeled off her life-jacket and parka, stripping down to the lightweight wet-suit she wore beneath.

She had meant only to toss her discarded clothes onto the nearby seat, but somehow they slid over the stern and into the sea. Not that she really cared. The feverish heat in her body told her she would not need them again. Neither did she need any more to eat. She threw the tin aside and that also slipped over the stern.

As it sank through the sunlit depths, something moved towards it: a long sleek form that butted the strange object with its nose before spiralling upwards. A glistening grey arc broke the surface, like a perfect miniature of the great whale body she had glimpsed beneath the boat during the storm. And abruptly a whole school of dolphins was playing around the boat. Leaping and diving, they cut zigzag paths across each other's wakes, leaving behind a thin tracery of bubbles that glittered and shone.

Somewhere in the coolness of the waning day, she could hear someone laughing; and she guessed it was herself, glad not to be alone any longer.

Then, just as suddenly as the dolphins had arrived, they

were gone, and it was late evening, merging into night. Habit told her she should go below, lie down on the bunk and sleep. And she truly believed that was what she had done – until she woke from a dream in the middle of the night and discovered she was still lying in the open, her body bathed in sweat.

In the dream she had been swimming amongst the dolphins, their round eyes watching her curiously as she dived with them down into the blue depths, the sea cool and soothing on her bare skin. By contrast, the night felt hot and sticky, the watchful stars much less friendly than her animal companions. So she quickly closed her eyes and willed herself back into the dream, leaving the loneliness and discomfort of the waking world far behind.

She was not sure when she next woke. The painful throbbing in her leg returned and she sat up and looked out across a sea as flat and smooth as a lake. The sun was high, beating down mercilessly, the atmosphere stiflingly hot, as was she. There was no sign of the dolphins. The only movement was in the sea immediately around the boat, where she could detect the constant swirls and eddies of an ocean current that was bearing her towards the south. But why there? she wondered hazily.

For no reason that she could explain, she recalled how the humpback whale had risen beneath her, as though using its great body to buffet the boat off course, away from the land. It had been replaced by its dolphin cousins, their

11

much smaller bodies swimming easily in and out of her dreams. She shook her head in confusion. Had they also been directing her, she asked herself, and should she follow?

Just asking the question was enough. It wasn't like being at home, with parents advising her or ordering her about. Here, there was only the windless day, the air grown furnace-hot, clinging to her skin like flame. And in response to the unbearable heat, she leaned out over the side.

Within arm's reach the sea glittered enticingly, as if urging her on; but as a precaution she took a short coil of rope from beneath the cockpit, tied one end to a stern-post, and flung the other end into the sea. Before she followed it, she paused briefly, amazed at her own audacity. Then she was plunging straight down into the placid blue of another world, exactly as in the dream. And as in the dream, all the unbearable heat left her body. Even the pain in her leg dissolved away, leaving her free to twist and turn as she pleased.

High above, she could see the rope, a thin white tentacle trailing behind the boat. The sight of it aroused an earlier fear, of being left behind, abandoned, and she shot hastily to the surface. But to her relief she found that the current was bearing her along too; she and the boat drifting southwards together.

12   She ceased to worry after that. Like the boat, she gave

herself to the ocean, satisfied by its silky cool touch. For what seemed to be hours, she swam lazily to and fro or dived deep; sinking down to where the sunlight barely reached and she was surrounded by soft darkness, her ears filled with the sound of her own heartbeat.

It was during one of these dives that she first became aware of an icy chill welling up from the depths. She shivered and stared into the formless gloom. At the limits of her vision she could see something moving: a large shadowy body swimming as lazily as she. Yet watchful, and drawing always nearer.

She recognised instantly what it was. The sleek head, the jutting dorsal fin, could have belonged to only one creature. A shark! Again she was caught in an upsurge of icy water that made her whole body shake with cold, and she turned in panic and arrowed up towards the boat hovering there in the calm blue of the day.

Always, during previous dives, the boat had remained floating above her, as if waiting. Yet now, while she was still struggling to reach the surface, it began drifting away, drawn on by the warm current, leaving her in the clutches of this much colder water that had lured the shark from the depths.

With silver bubbles billowing from her mouth, she kicked out desperately, fearful that at any moment the toothed mouth would snatch at her legs. The surface rushed to meet her and she burst free. Out into an ocean much wider and emptier than she remembered. A desolate blue waste in which she was no more than a tiny speck. Frantically, she swung around, searching. The boat was already out of reach, but the end of the rope was still swishing past, and she lunged and caught it with both hands.

As she was tugged along, half-buried in a smother of foam, she glimpsed the shark from the corner of her eye, its dorsal fin cutting the water over to her right. Purposely, she jack-knifed her body, driving herself under; and through a froth of bubbles and sun-streaked water, she saw the streamlined body swimming parallel to her own. Idly flicking its tail, it veered in towards her, one expressionless eye observing her coldly as it slid beneath her exposed belly and half-turned.

'No!' she screamed out, not to the air and sky, but to the vast watery spaces of the ocean. 'Get away!'

Her cries seemed to go no further than herself; to be swallowed up by the blue-black emptiness. And again the shark was sliding beneath her, its rough sandpaper skin rasping against her legs as it passed. Shuddering from the contact, she surfaced long enough to gulp in air and then jack-knifed down once more, convinced that if she took her eyes off the creature for more than a few seconds it would strike.

The rope was biting into her palms now, her arms and shoulders aching from the effort of holding on. There was also the cold to contend with, her limbs growing stiff and unresponsive. So that when the shark angled in for the third time, she could not kick out in self-defence, even though it slowed as it brushed against her: its body as icy cold as the surrounding water; its tail slapping her aside with cruel playfulness.

'Help me,' she murmured softly, as if pleading with the ocean itself. 'Please make it go away.'

The only response, more heartless even than the silence, was the appearance of another dark shape swimming up from the deep. It was bigger than the shark – longer, far

15

bulkier – and moving with strangely ponderous speed.

This new danger was more than she could bear. Choked with terror, she clawed at the rope, lost her grip entirely, and surfaced in a flurry of foam.

Immediately the shark closed in, its dorsal fin cutting a straight, deadly line through the water. But before it could reach her, something glittered and broke far beneath them – a succession of bubbles that exploded from the dark shape swimming below and spun upwards. The bubbles reached the surface in long thin lines, like strings of silvery beads; a curtain of them that formed a protective circle around her helpless body.

Although that enclosing circle was made of nothing but air, the shark was unwilling to enter it. As it halted its rush and slanted away, several smaller shapes followed the ascending bubbles. Their tails pumping energetically, they drove at the shark, scaring it off; their beak-like mouths issuing excited, clicking cries as they leaped gracefully from the water.

Claire felt one of the bodies rise gently beneath her, its skin unexpectedly warm, reassuring. Just as gently, it bore her across the surface towards the boat and floated there while she reached up with trembling hands and gripped the side.

Only when she was safely on board did she fully realise what had happened. And by then the dolphins, their job done, had disappeared. The bulky shape far below had also

gone, back into the darkness from which it had come. Though she knew it now for what it was: not a shark at all, but a great whale, the air from its lungs forming the net of bubbles that had saved her.

Perhaps because she had read about those glittering circles of bubbles, she was not surprised. 'Thank you,' she whispered through chattering teeth. And with her chilled body pressed against the hot planking, she drifted back into unconsciousness.

CHAPTER THREE

Riding the Whale

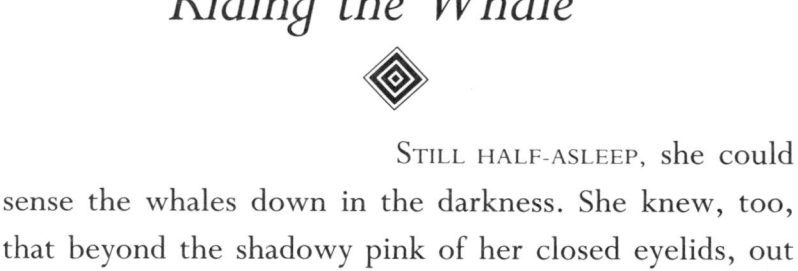

STILL HALF-ASLEEP, she could sense the whales down in the darkness. She knew, too, that beyond the shadowy pink of her closed eyelids, out there in the bright day, their massive backs would be breaking the surface of the ocean, their spouts misting the sunlight. One of them must have risen close to the boat, because she felt a cool wash of spray on her fevered skin. So refreshing that she could not resist it; and despite the persistent pain in her leg, which made her moan aloud each time she moved, she hauled herself up onto the stern.

The whale, a fully grown humpback, was still floating alongside: its body a shiny black hillock; its flippers, immensely long and knobbly on the front edge, like giant oars jutting from its body. It rolled half onto its side for a better view of her, one huge low-set eye regarding her with a strange air of understanding. As though in sympathy

18

with what it saw – her face and neck badly sunburned and
blistered – it blew again: the spray, smelling of the sea and
its many tiny creatures, drifting over her as before.

'Yes!' she gasped. 'Yes!' And lifted her face thankfully
to the fine mist.

Beside her, the eye, the long head and body, submerged
in a welter of foam. The vast black-and-white flukes were
all that remained, poised above the surface; and then they
too descended, thwacking the water so hard that the
resulting wave drenched her.

19

She had no need to make any conscious decision. Like the water running from her hair and skin, she slipped easily over the stern and into the blissfully cool embrace of the sea. It accepted her as if she were no longer a creature of the earth, the silvery surface closing over her head, the whale's turbulent wake drawing her down.

Some way ahead, through the sun-dappled blue, a blurred shape was swimming with a slow undulating motion. It grew still as she strained towards it, floating there in the watery space, waiting patiently. She closed the gap with a few strokes, diving beneath the tail to where the white undersides were blotched with barnacles and fragments of trailing weed. Further along, from the middle of the belly to the extent of the thrusting jaw, the whitened skin was ridged with even lines of pleats – long grooves pressed into the pale flesh. Wonderingly she reached up to touch them.

But that was testing the animal's patience too far, and with a shuddering roll it flicked her with one of its long side-flippers. There was no aggression in the action. It was the gentlest of movements, yet still she was sent tumbling down and down to where the sunlight ended and the blackness began.

Below her, the murky heart of the ocean waited, more watchful than ever. On this occasion no sinister shapes circled in the shadows; no icy water gusted up to where she hovered. Even so, she did not care to linger there.

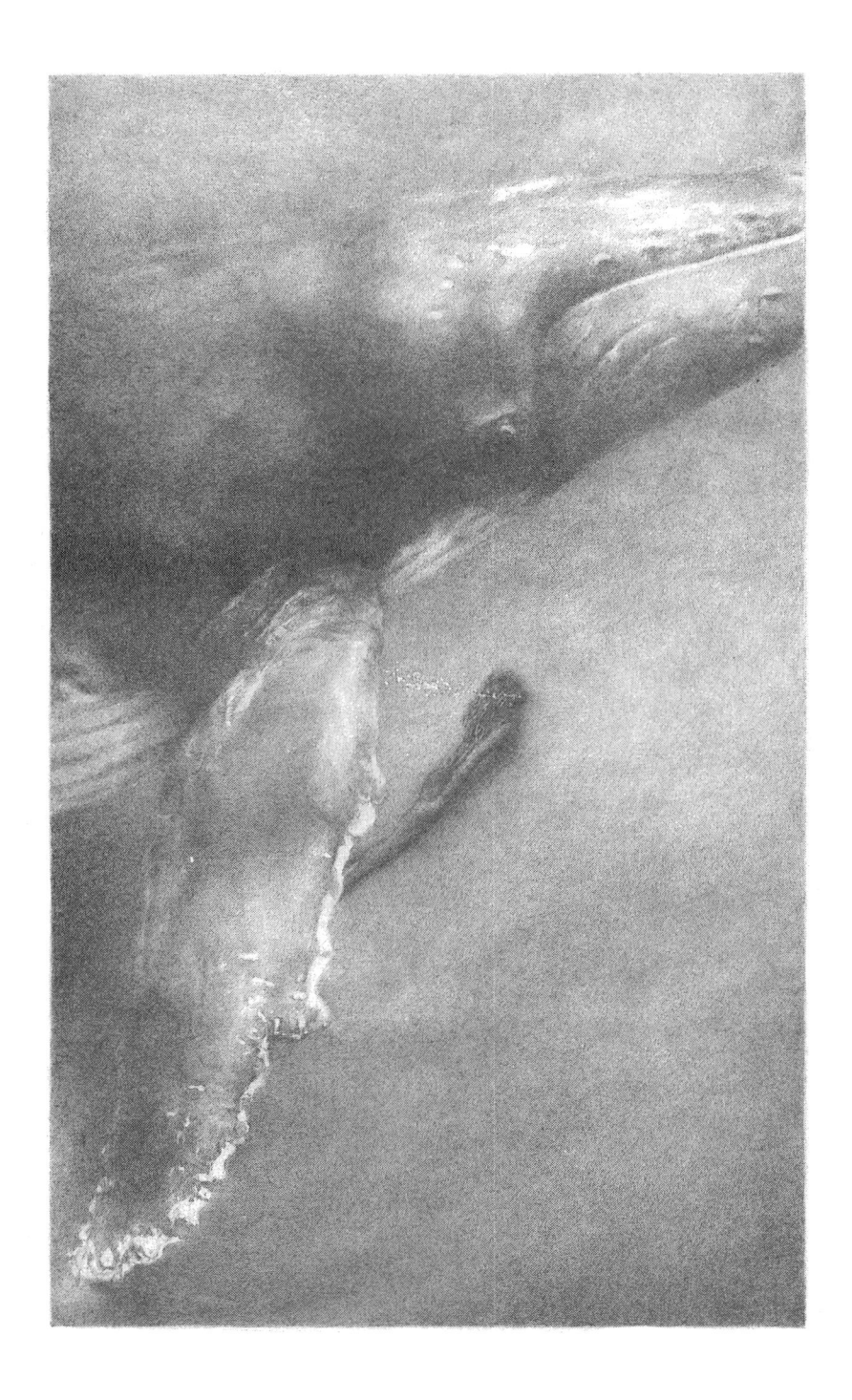

The memory of the shark was too fresh. And she turned and kicked upwards, filling her aching lungs with fresh clean air as she broke clear.

By her own calculation she could not have been under for more than a minute or so; but in that time the day had been transformed. A sharp wind had sprung up, the beginnings of a swell already appearing; while overhead the blue sky was giving way to a haze of cloud.

The suddenness of the change was enough in itself to alarm her, and she looked around for the boat. It was no longer close by. Driven by the wind, it was nearly a hundred metres away, its bows dipping into the low swell.

As with her encounter with the shark, she nearly panicked. Instead of conserving her energy, she began thrashing at the water in a frantic attempt to close the gap.

And close it she did, surprisingly quickly. For as she soon realised, the boat was not being pushed forward by the wind. It had merely been blown sideways, she and the boat still held by the strong current, both of them still being carried southwards at the same rate.

Relieved, she trod water while she caught her breath. And now that she was calm, she saw something else that reassured her. The whales had not left: their spouts, like friendly signals, jetted skywards on every side. Wherever she looked, mountainous backs curved into view. She was swimming in the very midst of the pod which was also heading south, keeping pace with the boat.

One of the whales passed almost beneath her, the wash sucking her under. Another much smaller shape followed: a calf swimming in its mother's wake. Unlike the mother, it checked its forward movement at the sight of her: its long-jawed head lifting to where she hung in the clear blue; its eyes gleaming through the pale light, as if in recognition. When it seemed that the giant face must collide with hers, it swerved slightly and, as inquisitive as any puppy, drifted past so close that one of the piebald flippers brushed her arm.

This brief contact was an invitation that she accepted readily, stretching out with both hands and grasping the knobbly edge of the flipper. The young animal did not quiver or shy away as the adult whale had done earlier. There was an eerie, inviting cry from the mother, calling the calf to her side, and all at once Claire was being dragged forward, the flipper softly pulsing beneath her hands.

A few seconds later the calf surfaced for air. As well as filling her own lungs, Claire used the opportunity to transfer her grip to the small dorsal fin on the animal's back. In that position, half-lying, half-sitting astride the broad body, she was swept under once again.

They went deeper than before, to the brink of the darkness that she usually feared. Though not now. Not with the mother's cries reaching them from above, calling them back up. Obedient but unhurried, the calf rose through lightening shades of blue to where the wind was whipping the tops from newly formed waves and the sky had grown leaden-grey.

Gulping in more air, she had to suppress a shiver, as though this world of wind and low cloud were really what she needed to fear. Then they were plunging back into the calm of a sea whose soft blue folds preserved the vanished warmth of the day.

For some time after that they rose and sank with a rhythm that Claire found peculiarly comforting; she and the calf snatching breaths at the same regular intervals; their heartbeats, like their bodies, attuned to each other. The periods up there in the day, where the wind sang across the boat's hull, were so brief that soon she found she could almost ignore them. The rest, the slow movement through the moist underworld, gradually took on the likeness of a dream, of a long sleep, in which the pain in her leg faded away, as did the lingering fever-heat of her body, leaving her with a sense of peace and silence.

Only one sound penetrated the silence: the mother whale's inviting voice, high-pitched, calling to her calf each time they sounded. Always it responded with a faint bleat of its own and with a brief surging motion. Except for once, when the mother's cry was a little more urgent, a little more insistent. The change in the tone was so slight that Claire failed to notice it. But the calf registered the

difference immediately, and instead of swimming up to the

mother's tail, it dived beneath the protective bulk of her body, searching for the nipple.

The next cry to reach them spoke so clearly of alarm that even Claire realised something was amiss. Low and booming, it came from some distance away – from a whale swimming on the outer fringes of the pod. And without hesitation both mother and calf plummeted in a steep dive, dragging Claire with them.

She was rushing through darkness, her head threatening to burst from the increased pressure, before she had the presence of mind to let go. High, high above, like a tiny silver-grey circle at the far end of a tunnel, she could see the sky. She climbed towards it, thrusting aside the thick water, following the trail of gleaming bubbles that leaked from her mouth and raced on ahead. In the last few metres she almost caught up with them. Her body shooting up and slicing through the mirror-surface . . . to where someone else was already waiting, watching for her appearance!

She saw the figure as she was drawing in her first gasping breath. Someone more or less her own size, floating between her and the boat. The head and shoulders, like her own, bobbed above the surface; the face, no less startled than hers, stared wide-eyed back at her.

'Who . . . ?' she half-shouted, and realised it was not a person at all, but a seal; and that its round eyes were

25

not just startled, but glazed with terror.

That brief act of recognition was all she had time for. One moment the seal was there; the next, it was swallowed up in a great eruption of water. In its place there was a much larger head and shoulders: a tooth-rimmed mouth still gaping; a powerful, neckless torso, with precise black-and-white colouring, outlined against the sky.

Her recognition of this other creature was instant-aneous.

'Orca!' she breathed out – using the name she had seen printed in books, beneath illustrations of killer whales.

The creature crashed sideways back into the water, sending out a ripple of wavelets that reached to where she floated. Others of its kind were swimming near by, their dorsal fins speeding across the surface.

She did not try and escape. If the seal had simply given up and waited for death, what chance did she have? She, who had none of the seal's swimming skills; who was trapped here, near the surface, by her constant need for air – the same air that now struck cold upon her cheeks and neck.

Some of that unfeeling cold seemed to invade the surrounding sea, and she glimpsed another black-and-white shape hurtling up from below. There was no time for terror. She felt a sickening lurch of dread as she braced herself for the sheer force of the impact. And a split-second later the danger had come and gone. Instead of a cruel and bloody mouth erupting where she had once been, there was a gentle parting of the waters close beside her; a bullet head angling from the surface; an open mouth, with a huge tongue lolling against the lower rim of dagger-teeth, as if the orca were laughing at her – sharing with her the pleasure of its discovery that she was not a seal, there simply to be eaten. Its orca mind fascinated by her slender limbs and her helplessness, and also by a mysterious sense of fellow-feeling.

It uttered a few clicking cries, and one of its companions rose beneath her and buoyed her up on its blunt forehead. She balanced there as the orca swam, head held high, through the heaving swell to where the rest of the pack waited. It released her then and, nervously to begin with, she swam amongst them, nudged this way and that by the tender pressure of their large bodies. A baby, hardly longer than herself, mouthed her arm with teeth that could easily have sheared through her soft flesh; yet it left behind only the faintest pattern of toothmarks that quickly faded. She

27

tried to follow it as it swam away, but she was too slow. And too cold and tired – her time in the water and her recent shock starting to take their toll.

Over to her right the boat continued its slow drift, bows to the wind, and she began swimming towards it. Several of the orcas, thinking she was confused, nudged her around, pointing her back towards the southern horizon where the cloud hung especially low and steel-grey. But when she insisted on turning aside, they seemed to grasp her purpose. One of them (the one that had lifted her earlier?) butted her forward, half-raising her from the water, pushing her along.

For the orca, their progress must have been slow. To Claire – a miniature bow-wave riding up her chest and splashing into her face – it felt as if they were racing along. The boat rushed to meet them, dropping into a trough as they approached, so they were almost level with the rail. A casual toss of the orca's head was all that was needed, and she was pitched over the rail and down into the cockpit.

When she rose and looked out, the whole pack had gathered about the boat, heads up, mouths agape as if in laughter. She wanted to join in, despite the desolate wastes of ocean all around; but the wind was too cold, like ice on her exposed skin, and she huddled down.

She did not hear them swim away. Nor, when she peered over the rail and found them gone, did she feel abandoned.

28

In her tired, fuddled state, it was as if the boat itself had taken on the likeness of a whale – she clinging to its back as it rode the swells; sucking in her breath each time it teetered on a crest. Even the wind had become a familiar voice, calling to her, beckoning her southwards.

CHAPTER FOUR

A Debt Repaid

◈

SHE DID NOT want to take refuge in the cabin. It wasn't just the water and debris washing about the floor that worried her, but the darkness, which reminded her too vividly of the ocean depths where the sun never reached. On the other hand, up there in the cockpit it had become bitterly cold. And with her parka and the rest of her clothes gone, she finally gave in and went below. Though not to stay. Only to refill her water-bottle and to change into a thicker wet-suit kept stored in one of the lockers.

It hurt her leg changing wet-suits, and she had to bite her lip so as not to cry out. Yet the thicker rubbery material did give some support to her damaged knee, and she was soon much warmer, even comfortable enough to sleep.

At least she thought she had been asleep, for when she

30

opened her eyes she felt rested, and the humpback whales had returned. She could hear their singing just by pressing her ear to the decking. Their voices, mingling with the wind that howled around the boat, spoke to her of contentment, even of joy.

With difficulty, her body strangely weak out there in the light and air, she grasped the side rail and sat up. The sea, like the sky, had turned from blue to steel-grey; and the low swells had grown into steeply sloping walls of water that foamed and boiled along their crests. In these cold, colourless wastes, there seemed to be no place for life and warmth, and she almost huddled back down. What held her there was the sudden appearance of an albatross, riding the storm with carefree abandon. Its long wings tipped trustingly to the wind, it slid over the nearest crest and banked sharply, its breast feathers only a hand's breadth from the water as it swooped along the inward curve of the trough. She glimpsed its eyes as it sailed past, so clear and bright, so devoid of fear; eyes that found nothing alien about these wild surroundings.

The whales were the same, totally at home here. Not just swimming, but frolicking in the rough seas; the spent air exploding from their lungs as if in triumph; their bodies, shiny black, filled with untold energy, heaving clear of the grey water in an open display of joy.

Even the boat showed every sign of belonging in these waters. It was dancing ahead of each breaking crest and dropping abruptly to where its bows plunged into the grey swell – only to shake itself free, with water pouring from its decks, and climb easily back into the wind. Again and again it emerged from the deep sea valleys unscathed, its up-and-down motion so familiar that when a whale rose alongside, Claire automatically loosened her hold on the rail and slipped into the sea.

There, at that moment, it somehow felt the natural thing for her to do. To move from the chill, noisy region of the wind into the warm silence of the waves; to abandon the flimsy shell of the boat, a thing of wood and metal, and choose instead a creature of flesh and blood.

And this time the whale accepted her completely. A faint shudder passed through it as she clung hard to its dorsal fin, but that was all. Its blow-hole winked shut and it pitched forward into the advancing swell, parting the waters so cleanly that Claire felt the merest tug. Then she was moving once more through a world of stillness, where the only sounds were the eerie voices of the whales calling to each other.

Above her, the long slopes of the waves drifted past, the boiling crests like blossoms of cloud in an otherwise silver sky. Angling upwards, they broke briefly through that sky, out into noise and confusion, and descended again, back to where peace reigned.

Another whale moved up from the lower realms of shadow and she transferred her grip – kicking free of one

giant body and fastening herself to another. It also accepted her presence, letting out a lowing cry of welcome; each upward lift of its tail bringing their bodies into momentary contact.

She could see other whales now: bulky shapes that glided with surprising grace through the gloom ahead. Whenever one drew near, she would swim towards it, her arms outstretched. And always her newly chosen companion would slow down and wait, floating patiently until it felt her hands tighten about its dorsal fin.

She was left behind only once, when she lost her grip and slipped back, the beating of the giant tail tossing her towards the surface. But she was not abandoned there for long. Before the crest of the next wave could reach her, there was a moaning call, half of welcome, half distress, and a heavily barnacled head lifted her clear. For a second or two she actually stood on the flat upper jaw. She took several quick steps backwards and was swept off her feet by the rush of water. But by then she was secure again, her hands clamped around the dorsal fin as the wave passed harmlessly above them.

She had no idea how long she had been swimming when she spied the calf. She heard its squealing cry, high and joyful, and it came hurrying towards her, its chunky body pumping vigorously. The mother, as always, was hovering in the background, her white underside faintly luminous in the poor light that fell like a blue-grey curtain to where they swam. She called to them, urging them higher, as Claire wrapped her legs around the calf's body and held on tightly.

It was as well that she did, for the young animal, overjoyed at this unexpected reunion, began cavorting wildly – twisting and diving, breaching in a flurry of spray and surfing down the long swells.

Because of the rush of water past her ears, Claire could hear the mother only faintly, her distant, mewing cries half-lost in the excitement of the moment. That was why the initial alarm went unnoticed. The first inkling she had that something was amiss was when the calf suddenly jerked and slewed around. The low voices of the bulls were booming out by then, warning of danger.

Claire, clinging on still, glanced nervously about her. The surface waters, which only minutes earlier had been thronged with vast blurry shapes, had become abruptly empty. Unnervingly so. The stillness no longer peaceful, but filled with nameless threat. Of all the humpback pod, only one adult remained in view: the mother, a brush-stroke of shadow far below, calling to them plaintively.

A tremor shook the calf's body and it dipped its head and drove downwards. But even before Claire could relax her hold, another dark form passed between them and the mother. A killer whale, the distinctive white markings reflecting the dim light.

Their escape route cut off, the calf lunged for the

surface – but other killer whales already waited there, black silhouettes against the silver sky. More of them patrolled on every side, circling slowly.

Entirely surrounded, the calf grew unnaturally still – Claire continuing to crouch on its back. They were both watching one orca in particular: a large male that was steadily closing in. Her lungs bursting, Claire longed to float free, to rise up to where she could suck in the cold, life-giving air; but she knew that if she deserted the calf now, it would be dead in seconds.

It was almost a relief when the orca began its charge, coming at them in a fast, shallow curve, its mouth open, ready to tear flesh from bone. She had only an instant in which to act, and quickly she threw back her head and let out a wordless shriek. The bubbles gushing from her mouth obscured her vision momentarily, so she did not see the way the orca balked at the sight of her – the sudden image of her limbs twined about the calf's mottled body causing it to check its charge and skim away. She glimpsed it passing over her shoulder, one pectoral fin brushing her cheek. And then she was pulling at the calf, urging it to rise.

Luckily, they surfaced in the calm water at the very base of a trough. With the calf blowing beside her, her first desperate gasp took in more steam than air. But as her breathing steadied, she noted with approval that the orcas showed no sign of renewing their attack. They were still circling dangerously, but holding off while she remained with the calf.

Encouraged, she took an extra-deep breath and bore down on the calf's head. It responded half-heartedly, too stupefied with fright to do more than duck beneath the oncoming wave. Again she leaned forward and pushed at the flattened upper jaw: and this time it began to swim down sluggishly. Several of the orcas accompanied them for a while, peeling off one by one as they sank deeper. At the point where the light gave way to blackness, only one big male remained, the last of their dangerous escort. Her head almost splitting from the pressure, Claire watched him also spiral away. Though still she hung on, wanting to be sure that the calf was truly safe.

Go! she kept urging it silently, for its movements remained sluggish. Go!

In answer to her voiceless pleading, a mewing cry sounded from the deep. And with one powerful thrust of its tail, the calf broke Claire's grip and vanished.

She was left floundering in the blackness, her head throbbing so violently from the pressure that she no longer knew which way was up and which was down. Slowly, more sluggish than the petrified calf, she groped her way through the gloom. Magically, it seemed, a light appeared before her, but too dim and distant ever to be reached. It was better, perhaps, to go on drifting here, on this borderline between day and night.

She had almost stopped swimming when the orcas arrived. Twirling about her, the slight pressure of their bodies jostling her into wakefulness, they bore her upwards. She neither helped nor resisted them, her arms too slack and weak to fend them off even had she wanted to. Through half-closed eyes, she could see the light expanding, brightening; but the darkness within her was stronger, drawing her to itself much as the mother whale had enticed her young.

She retained no memory of reaching the surface; nor of clambering back into the boat. When she awoke it was night, the sky clear and black and speckled with stars. The wind blew as fiercely as ever, shrieking insanely as it buffeted the tiny boat, heaving it from side to side. In all that noise and motion, it was impossible for any other voice to reach her. Yet now, without needing to be told, she understood why she was there. She, like the whales, was caught up in a great journey to the southern oceans. Where something awaited her. Some special purpose that . . .

But again she slept.

CHAPTER FIVE

Intruder

SHE MUST HAVE been ill for a while. Waking and sleeping fitfully, she was vaguely aware of days passing and of the boat driving on beneath her. Sometimes, half-awake, she would hear the whales calling far below, their melodious voices oddly in keeping with the moan of the wind and the gurgle of water along the sides. Even asleep she was conscious of their distant song, the long wailing notes reaching her through a haze of darkness and mist.

That same mist continued to shroud the day when she finally recovered. It was light, but with no sign of the sun. The sky was an oppressive roof of cloud that glowed dully. Lower portions of cloud, like flimsy strips of muslin or lace, were peeling away and curling lazily past the boat, so that often she felt as if she were adrift in the sky. Only the thrusting motion, as the boat scurried down the long swells, reminded her of where she truly was: the surrounding sea as limitless as ever; the following waves still mountainously high. Though now that the wind had slackened, the tops of the crests were softly rounded and no longer ridged with foam.

Listlessly, she reached for the water-bottle and was surprised to find it empty, for her lips were cracked and dry and caked with salt. She was equally surprised to find how weak she had grown. She had to make several attempts just to stand up; and the climb down into the cabin, to refill the bottle, was almost beyond her.

Back in the cockpit, the musty taste of stored water easing the soreness in her throat, she rested for a while before clambering onto the stern. That also taxed her strength. Yet it was worth the effort, because she felt better, stronger, the moment she released her hold and rolled sideways into the welcoming sea.

Compared with the clammy touch of the mist, the sea was warm. And unlike the deck, it was soft, exerting a gentle upward pressure that supported her full weight. Floating free, one hand holding lightly to the trailing rope, she could feel her lost strength returning; the contained energy of the waves somehow flowing into her limbs, healing her.

At her first dive, she saw the calf: a familiar mottled shape waiting patiently beneath the waves. She tried to copy its mewing cry as it hurried to meet her – and may well have been successful, because when the mother loomed out of the background dark, she showed no hint of nervousness; her barnacle-encrusted snout nuzzling them both lovingly.

As before, Claire was soon drawn into the communal life of the pod. In company with the calf – sometimes clinging to its fin, sometimes swimming unaided – she moved easily amongst the great rising and dipping bodies. The way the adults watched her with their large soulful eyes, so trustingly, made her feel as if she were also a calf. Their snoring sighs, their repetitive song, might have been aimed directly at her, like some previously unknown language she was rapidly learning to understand. Certain sounds she recognised as offering encouragement; others as expressing care and concern; others again, more strident and demanding, obviously warned of danger.

It was a series of such warning cries that sent her shooting to the surface; the rest of the pod diving deep, down into that icy darkness she dared not enter.

As she had suspected, the orcas were the cause of the alarm: their angled fins, their piebald backs, clearly visible near the crest of the oncoming wave. But this time it was not the humpbacks they were after. Far up the opposite side of the same wave there was a flash and glitter of darting bodies. Seals! Fleeing desperately from the hunters.

Infected by the fever of the hunt, the orcas spared her only a brief greeting as they sped past. She barely had time to return their greeting before they disappeared, leaving her alone.

Alone, but not lonely. Because she knew that the whales would soon be back. Also, some inner sense warned her that for the time being at least the calf was safe. In the immediate future it was not the orcas it needed to fear, but . . . But what?

She shivered, suddenly unsure, and reached for the rope trailing in the water near by. Looping it about her waist, she let it drag her slowly along; calmed, lulled almost into a state of sleep, by the steady movement. Content to drift on until she was startled into alertness by the horn-like calls of the adult humpbacks; and the squat outline of the calf reappeared beneath her, matching its body movements to hers.

She rejoined it eagerly, sinking down into the friendly half-lit area beneath the waves. The two of them swimming together as if nothing had happened to disturb them. The calf's smooth body pressed warmly against her own.

Yet not warmly enough. For every so often she was overtaken by a fresh fit of shivering – the cold coming not from below, but filtering down from above. The glittering surface like a sheet of ice that made her gasp every time they broke through; the air knife-sharp on her wet skin, cutting into her lungs with each breath.

More than ever she was thankful to duck back down; preferring to hold her breath until she was dizzy rather

41

than urge the calf up to where the light shone icily upon the sleek banks of passing waves. And with practice she found she could stay down for longer and longer periods, as if her body were accustoming itself to this watery underworld.

How long she swam with the calf she was never sure. Hours? Days? Even afterwards, looking back, it was hard for her to estimate the exact time. All she could recall clearly was the steady rocking motion that never stopped; the whales' song filling the grey-blue emptiness . . . and the encroaching cold. Always the cold. Numbing her flesh. Seeping into her bones. So that no matter how tightly she clung to the calf's warm young body, still she could not keep the deep chill at bay. Her limbs growing stiff with it; her teeth chattering until her jaw ached.

Eventually it was the cold that drove her back to the boat. Unable to hold on any longer, she floated free of the calf and rose helplessly. The animal followed for a while, calling sadly as it spiralled about her. Other, much larger whales, responding to its cries, slid from the shadows: giant creatures that watched her depart with an air of regret, their trumpeted song imploring her to stay. But she was too feeble now to do more than drift up to a surface that glinted like frosted glass.

She crashed through it in a shower of icy droplets. Out into a world more dreary than she could have imagined. Colourless and empty. The sky leaden; the sea, arched with waves, reflecting back the same drab greyness. The mist, much thicker than before, had become a drapery of dirty white lace torn into fragments by the breeze.

And there was something else about the day that worried her. Something she could not pin down at first – though it made her glance uncertainly across her shoulder as she reached for the rope and pulled herself wearily from the water. It came to her then – that there was also a sinister quality about this dismal scene. As if some dangerous, hidden presence were waiting out there, preparing to strike.

Half-kneeling in the cockpit – blue with cold, her shoulders hunched and shaking – she peered nervously over the side. The character of the sea, she discovered, had begun to change. The long waves were no longer smooth, their surface unbroken. Now, bobbing ice-flows were appearing in the slack water of the troughs. Their number increased steadily as the day wore on: some small; some almost as big as the boat. Towards nightfall a particularly large flow – an iceberg in miniature – sailed over the nearest swell and bore down upon her. Tall and jagged, it jarred against the boat, grating and shrieking its way along the gunnel and making her cringe down onto the deck.

When she looked up the mist had closed in. A hazy white curtain, it hovered just beyond her reach, deadening every sound, reducing the boat's forward momentum to a dreadful stillness from which she feared it would never break.

She waited, ill at ease, shaking now from more than the cold. At last, gratefully, she felt a slight breeze on her cheek, and straight away the curtain of mist was split in two. But through the ragged tear, she saw not light and space: only something more sinister still. The kind of intruder she had never dreamed of sighting here. A dark shape in silhouette. A low-hulled ship passing across the near horizon, the throb of its motor reaching her through the silence.

Again she cringed back, not even tempted to call out for help. Because that one glimpse, before the mist closed and hid her from view, had been enough. She knew beyond all question what she had seen. No ordinary ship, but a whaler. The unmistakable shape of a harpoon-gun perched right up on the bow.

Hastily, she pressed her ear to the deck and listened. The low song and the throb of the engine sounded together. As did her own broken sob of distress. She could not help herself; could not keep silent as she knew she should. All she could think of was how the whales, at that very instant, might be spearing up towards the dying light. The calf amongst them. Its mottled back brushing aside the ice-flows as it surfaced. While near at hand the whaler lay in wait, its harpoon-gun trained upon the sea.

CHAPTER SIX

Journey's End

◈

WAKING WAS HARDER than usual. Like struggling up through ice-bound water towards a ring of frosty light. Groggily, her eyes still clouded with sleep, she emerged at last into a raw wintry day. Windless. The sea unnaturally calm. The air hazy with half-frozen mist. Through the mist, she could make out the blurred outline of vast phantom shapes. Icebergs. Some so tall that they towered above her, their peaks lost in cloud. In contrast to their ghostly whiteness, the stretches of open sea were dark blue merging into black, and mirror-smooth.

It was through that glassy smoothness, without warning, that a whale breached. A giant male humpback, it burst joyously through the surface, scattering water in mirror-fragments as it shot skywards. At its highest, the tip of its thrusting snout rivalled the icy peaks, all but its flukes clear of the water. With a sound like a gunshot, it blew

noisily, shattering the silence; and its great body, as it fell back, stirred the placid sea into foam and sent waves shuddering away.

Claire had barely recovered from her surprise when another adult male breached even closer to the boat, its whole body twisting in a kind of joyful dance before it flopped back. Within minutes that same dazzling display was repeated again and again as one male after another drove up vertically through the misty air and pirouetted upon its tail, its oar-like fins twirling freely.

All around the boat the sea was boiling and foaming. The boat had begun to rock wildly, as if it too were celebrating the whales' arrival at their feeding grounds. And Claire, looking on, had to cling to the handrail to prevent herself being flung against the sides of the cockpit.

Then, as suddenly as it had started, the display was over, and the whole pod settled to the business of feasting on the swarms of krill that populated these southern waters. Instead of breaching enthusiastically, they were now diving deep and releasing rings of bubbles that rose to the surface like circular nets in which countless tiny creatures milled about. The whales followed close behind: their cavernous mouths gulping in huge quantities of krill; the unwanted water pouring out through their massive jaw plates.

Like the whales, Claire was so caught up by their activity that for a while she was aware of nothing else. What first alerted her to possible danger was a vague suggestion of

movement somewhere out there in the mist. It was accompanied by a low hum that grew ever louder and became eventually the unmistakable throb of an engine.

She saw it then, for the second time: the dark outline of the whaler! The thing she had longed never to meet again; that she had hoped was merely a part of some bad dream. For surely whalers no longer existed. Surely! Wasn't that what she had read in books? In magazines? Yet there it was, passing across the narrow channel between two icebergs. As black as they were white, but no less ghostly. More hungry than any orca and far more deadly.

It was visible only for the space of a few breaths. She blinked and it was already fading, nosing its way back into the grey-white pall of mist. Though now she no longer doubted its reality. It was out there still, circling the peacefully feeding pod. She had only to turn her head to hear it: the throb of its engines like the beating of some heart of steel.

'Go away!' she screamed. And then, to the whales that continued to feed, unafraid: 'Leave me!' Because she preferred to be abandoned, left alone in all that cold wasteland, rather than have them fall to the harpoon.

But although her voice carried shrill and clear through the still air, it could not penetrate down through the glassy surface of the sea, to the swarming dark where the whales swam contentedly.

Again the whaler appeared, over to her right – a lean, wolfish look about its low-slung shape; its jutting prow armed not with teeth, but with the sinister shape of a mounted gun. She swung towards it; glimpsed a human figure on the prow; a human face peering intently along the gunsights. Never had she seen a face so unfeeling, eyes so empty of warmth. And she opened her mouth to protest, but once more the veil of mist drifted back, the ship and its harpooner fading to nothing.

She realised then that she had little time in which to act. The whales had to be warned. Painfully, because the ache in her leg had returned, she dragged herself up onto the stern, swung her feet over the edge . . . and stopped! She had been expecting to find the water cold, but not like this! So icy that it seemed to burn the skin of her bare feet, to penetrate instantly through the lower half of her wet-suit and chill her to the bone.

She knew she could not last long in such a temperature. A few minutes of full alertness was all she could hope for. After that, weakened, overcome by drowsiness, she would begin the slow drift into . . . No, not sleep. She understood well enough what awaited her down there. Hadn't she already encountered the shark, its lean body knifing up through waters as icy as these?

Instinctively, she drew her legs clear and pulled herself back on board. And it was then, while she was kneeling on the stern, undecided, that the whaler made its third and final appearance.

Some sixth sense warned her of its presence even before she heard it. The throbbing pain in her leg and the throb of the engine suddenly became one and the same. Behind her the mist parted, torn aside by an unseen hand: and there, coming straight towards her, was the knife-edge of the ship's prow. Above it stood the loaded gun; and above that again, the cold-eyed face staring past her.

She stumbled clumsily to her feet and began waving her arms frantically, but the harpooner seemed not to notice her. His eyes were fixed hungrily on the waters ahead, upon a scene she somehow knew by heart, without needing to turn and look – the blue-black surface of the ocean divided by the glistening arch of the female whale's body; and in her wake, within sight of the harpooner, the mottled, defenceless back of the calf.

This time Claire did not hesitate, entering the water in a long clean dive. The first shock of contact drove the breath from her lungs, forcing her up. Desperately, willing her freezing muscles to obey, she sucked in more air and dived again. The water all about her was murky with krill – thousands of the tiny creatures, like dust motes dancing in the dim light, which made it impossible to see more than a few metres ahead. But behind her the churning power of the engines was growing more distinct, and she

51

clawed at the shadows that hemmed her in; heaved with numb hands and arms until a much larger, moving shadow appeared out of the gloom.

The calf, as always, greeted her with a squeal of delight. She tried to answer it with a warning; but in her half-frozen condition she could manage no more than a feeble croak, the breath leaving her mouth in a slow dribble of bubbles. Already beginning to weaken, she grabbed for a side-fin and squirmed onto the animal's back; and the calf, thinking she was being playful, shot towards the surface.

It was the very worst thing that could have happened, because the mother immediately followed. All three of them marooned there in the bleak Antarctic day, with the whaler bearing down upon them.

From the corner of her eye, Claire glimpsed the man swinging the gun into position, steadying it for the shot. All her instincts demanded that she leap clear and save herself. Yet somehow she could not bring herself to do it. Why had she come here, she wondered briefly, if not for this? And to her own fearful astonishment, she stood up on the calf's flattened snout, placing her trembling body in the direct path of the harpoon.

She had barely straightened up when she heard the muffled crack of the harpoon being fired. It was accompanied by a yell as the man yanked at the gun, jerking the muzzle high in a frantic attempt to avoid hitting her. But with her eyes clenched shut, from sheer terror, she knew nothing of that. There was a whistle of something passing above her head; the whine and twang of heavy rope racing out; and then a dull boom as the head of the harpoon exploded harmlessly somewhere beneath the surface.

What saddened her afterwards was that she never had a chance to say goodbye. No sooner had the explosion sounded than the calf fell away from beneath her – both calf and mother dropping like stones into the safety of the depths. She was left floundering, while the whaler swept past, the turbulence of its wake sucking her under.

That nearly finished her, the violence of the undercurrents sapping her strength, drawing her down to where she lacked the will to resist. Entombed in the black krill-heavy sea, the cold like an iron clamp upon her lungs, she came close to losing her grip on that slender thread of belief that connected her to this place. With her heart labouring on in the darkness, she might almost have been anywhere – even closed up in the sightless regions of her own mind: an inner world that offered no easy escape;

where she could wander deeper and deeper, until the silence and the gloom became complete.

Yet if she was the one who had saved the calf, finally it was the calf that saved her. She never forgot that, in spite of all that people said later. For it was the calf's plaintive call, no one else's, which rose from the ocean floor and broke in upon her isolation: the young animal voice, like a bright light of sound, pointing her upwards; directing her through the maze of confusion and doubt, up to where the long Antarctic day lingered on.

She was only half-conscious when she surfaced. The whaler by then had disappeared, swallowed for ever by the mist. Feebly, past caring what happened to her, she swam back to the boat. Her limbs numb with cold, she dragged herself over the stern and into the cockpit.

Lying there, gazing up, she watched as the tall blue-white icebergs drifted past. The slow procession told her that the boat was moving again, caught up in the same current that had already brought her so far. At the thought of her journey continuing, a warm ray of hope entered her frozen body. It occurred to her that she might yet catch up with the whales and ride free on the back of the calf as she had before. There, where the southern ocean ended and all journeys began anew, she and the whales might . . .

Her one faint hope was destroyed a moment later, when the boat, after lurching noisily from side to side, came to a jarring halt. The impact pitched her half-way down the companionway and she had to crawl back. That was surprisingly easy, because the boat was now lying on its beam, having run aground on a flat shelf at the base of one of the icebergs.

Still shaking with cold, she grasped the side rail and lowered herself onto the ice. Above her rose a blue-white cliff that glistened and shone even in that misty atmosphere. So this, she thought calmly, is where it all ends. Here, in a shimmering ice-world.

Half-crawling, she made her way up a snowy incline and sat with her back to the cliff. From there, she had a wide view of the ocean. It appeared bluer than she remembered it. The mist had lifted, and while she watched, the clouds thinned, parted, and the sun filtered through, unexpectedly warm on her face. There was a stir of movement beneath the sea: high triangular fins, rounded at the top, were cutting cleanly through the water; hooped piebald backs disrupted the mirror-surface. She smiled and waved a greeting, gladdened by the way the orcas raised their voices in reply, piping happily as they sped past.

Satisfied at last, she leaned back and closed her eyes, giving herself to the sun's warmth and to the drowsiness that crept like slow flame through her chilled body. The last thing she heard as she fell asleep were the farewell cries of the orcas. Then she was plummeting, not into blackness, but into sun-streaked depths of unbroken dream, where the great whale shapes resumed their song and the calf swam joyfully from the shadows.

CHAPTER SEVEN

Saved

THE SUN WAS still warm on her face; but it was shining now through an open window whose silky white curtains were being lifted idly by the wind. She turned and saw a long room filled with beds, and it dawned on her that she was in a hospital. Someone was sitting close beside her, holding her hand; someone else bending over her pillow.

'She's coming round!' she heard her father say in an excited whisper.

And her mother's face, smiling with relief, dipped down towards her.

That was how she found out she had been saved. Though not until the next day did she feel strong enough to tell her story.

Propped up in bed, her broken leg encased in plaster, she described to her parents all that had happened –

starting with how she had cut away the mast and ending with the boat running aground on the ice. She left nothing out.

When she had finished, there was an embarrassed silence. Her mother coughed uncomfortably and looked out of the window.

'I know you think you're telling us the truth,' her father said gently. 'But really it couldn't have been like that, believe me. You just imagined it. You see, the chances are you were never more than a hundred kilometres from land. They found the boat washed up on the south coast. You'd managed to crawl ashore and were lying unconscious at the base of a cliff.'

The image of a tall, shimmering cliff of ice came back to her quite vividly, and she shook her head. 'No, it really happened,' she insisted. 'I was there, swimming with the whales. I saw it all. The shark and the calf and the whaling ship and . . . and everything.'

Her mother coughed again. 'You only *thought* you saw those things,' she murmured unhappily. 'You were delirious, that's all.'

'Delirious?'

'It was because you stayed in the open cockpit,' her father explained quickly. 'You suffered badly from exposure. There was the pain from your broken leg as well. Most of the time you wouldn't have known where you were.'

She felt too tired to go on arguing with them. What

57

would have been the use anyway? As far as she could tell, their minds were made up. According to her father, even something as solid and real as the whaling ship had to be an illusion. After all, hadn't the nations of the world given up whaling years before? There was also the problem of the icebergs: they only existed in Antarctic waters, far from where she had actually been. Or so he claimed.

'You might as well face up to it,' her mother concluded in a kindly voice. 'It all took place inside your head. Nowhere else. It was a wonderful dream, but a dream just the same. The kind of thing that sometimes happens to people in a high fever.'

Claire nodded, saying nothing, acting as if she were convinced. And she went on acting like that not only for the rest of the afternoon, but during their subsequent visits. As the days slipped by, it seemed so much easier simply to pretend that her parents were right; far easier than trying to answer all their objections. So that by the end of a week, when she was well enough to go home, it was more or less assumed that she had come round to their way of thinking.

'How's our whale girl today?' her mother asked jokingly when she arrived to collect her.

With a nurse's help, Claire eased herself from the bed down into a wheelchair. She was so glad to be leaving the hospital that she didn't mind being made fun of.

'Oh, about ready for another journey to the South Pole,' she answered.

They were still laughing together when her father drove up to meet them at the hospital entrance. She had not seen him for a couple of days and his face appeared unusually serious.

'So what are we waiting for?' her mother prompted him once Claire was settled comfortably in the back seat. 'Let's go home.'

He hesitated, one hand resting uncertainly on the ignition key, his eyes seeking out Claire's in the rear-view mirror.

'I've been down the coast to pick up the boat,' he explained. 'There are a few things that have me puzzled.'

'Is that a reason for sitting here outside the hospital?' her mother began laughingly. But then, noticing his expression, she grew equally serious. 'What is it?' she asked.

'Well, the boat was a bit of a wreck, as you'd imagine, but it was still intact. And it had a rope where Claire said it would: trailing from the stern-post. Exactly what you'd need if you were in the sea and wanted to climb back on board.' He paused and drew in his breath. 'I discovered something else as well. When they found Claire, she was wearing a heavy-duty wet-suit. They hadn't mentioned that before. Evidently it was stiff with salt. As though . . . as though she'd spent a lot of time in the water.'

'In the water?' her mother echoed him sharply. 'You mean swimming? But surely you don't . . .'

60

'Hold on,' he interrupted her, 'there's one last thing. Half an hour ago, before I came to pick you up, I rang Greenpeace. I was told there are still whaling ships. They're referred to as research vessels these days, but the fact is they still hunt whales.'

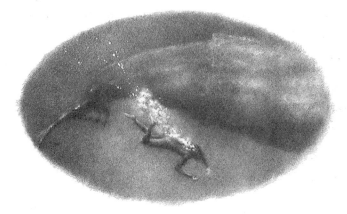

He swung around now and gazed straight at Claire. Her mother had also turned towards her. Both of them obviously troubled, doubtful, looking to their daughter for reassurance.

Once again she felt tempted to tell them what had actually happened. Then, all at once, she realised that there was no need to. Somehow it was sufficient just to know the truth; to be sure in her own mind of all that she had seen and done. Hadn't she shared the great southward journey of the humpback whales? One of the greatest journeys in the world? Wasn't that enough in itself?

She gave a deliberate shrug and lowered her eyes. 'It's like you said,' she answered dutifully. 'I was delirious most

61

of the time. I probably didn't have a clue about what was going on while I was out there in the boat.'

Yet that was not what she was thinking at all. Secretly, she was reliving her days and nights at sea: picturing to herself the bulky shapes of humpback whales gliding gracefully through the blue; hearing again the calf's last squealing call, an urgent voice directing her away from the blackness of doubt and disbelief, up towards the brightening day.

She blinked in the strong sunlight streaming through the side window of the car, suddenly aware of krill-like specks of dust floating in the air all about her.

'Yes,' she breathed contentedly. 'Anything could have happened while I was out there. Anything . . .'